Early Maths

For Preschool and Early Years

Illustrated by
Andy Cooke

www.autumnchildrensbooks.co.uk

Get ready to count...

When we have lots of things, we like to count them! But sometimes it's not so easy...

Octopus tried to count his legs, but he found it was a knotty problem.

Leopard tried to count his spots, but it made him see spots in front of his eyes!

Can you help Octopus count his legs and help Leopard count his spots? Point to the numbers and say them.

1
2
3
4
5
6
7
8
9
10

Buckle my shoe

There are rhymes to help Octopus and Leopard learn to count. Here's one of them.

1, 2, buckle my shoe.

3, 4, knock at the door.

5, 6, pick up sticks.

7, 8, lay them straight.

9, 10, a speckled hen.

How many eggs has the speckled hen laid?

Well done! Every time you finish a page, put your reward sticker here.

What can you see?

Count up to 3, what can you see?

Count up to 3 – birds in the tree.

Count up to 5 – bees in the hive.

Count up to 7 – stars in heaven.

Count up to 9 – clothes on the line.

Count 10 or more – shells on the shore.

How many shells on the shore?
Were there more than 10?

Counting down

Write the missing numbers for the countdown from 10 to 1.

Well done! Put your reward sticker here.

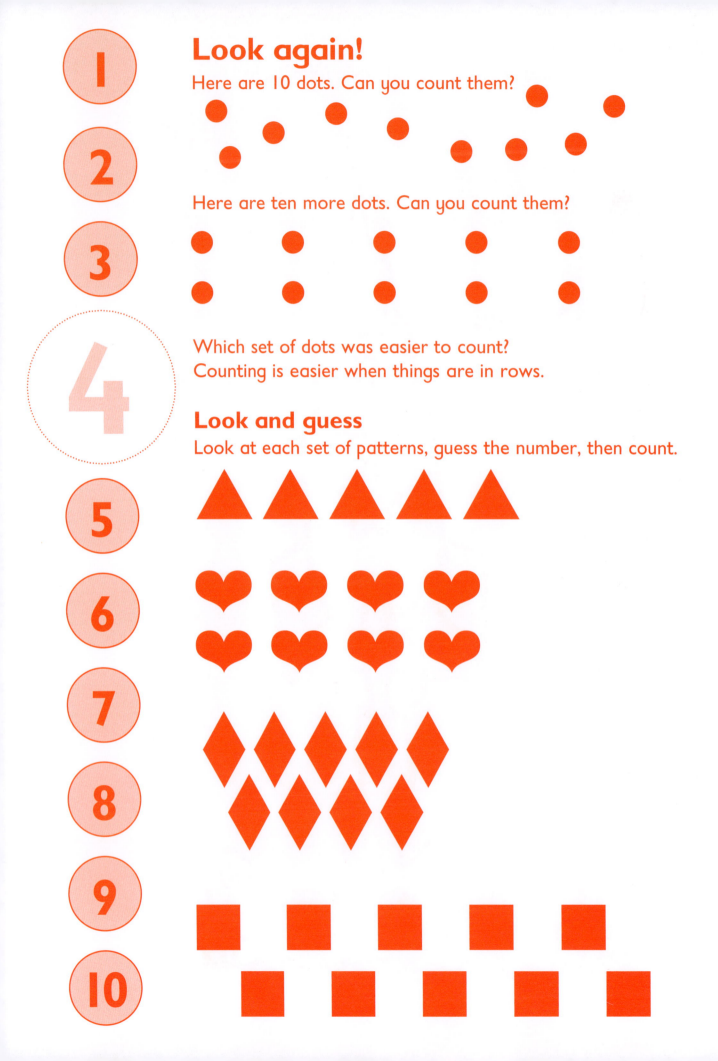

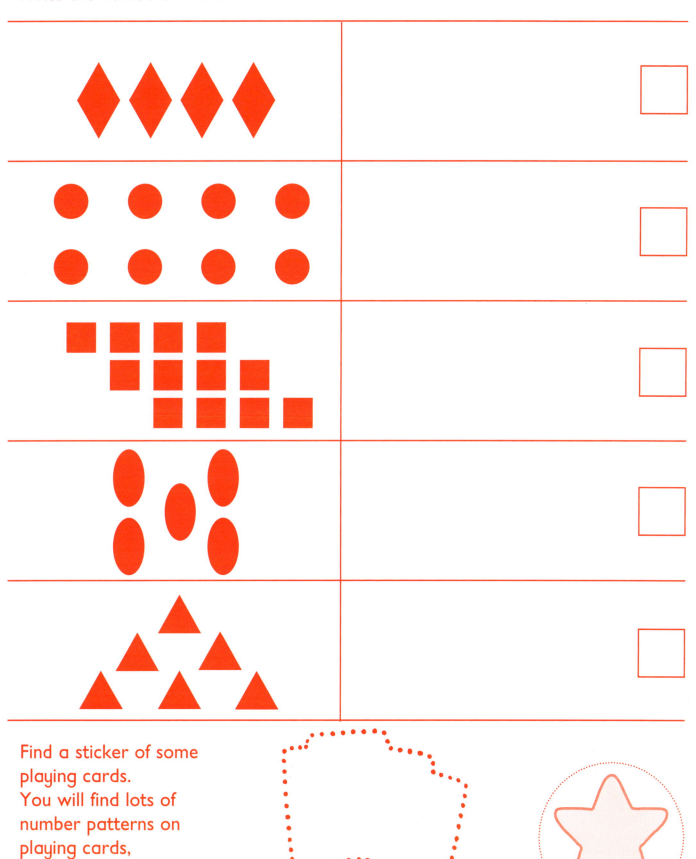

Number patterns
Copy each pattern. Then guess the number and count.
Write the numbers in the boxes.

Find a sticker of some playing cards. You will find lots of number patterns on playing cards, dominoes and dice.

Well done! Put your reward sticker here.

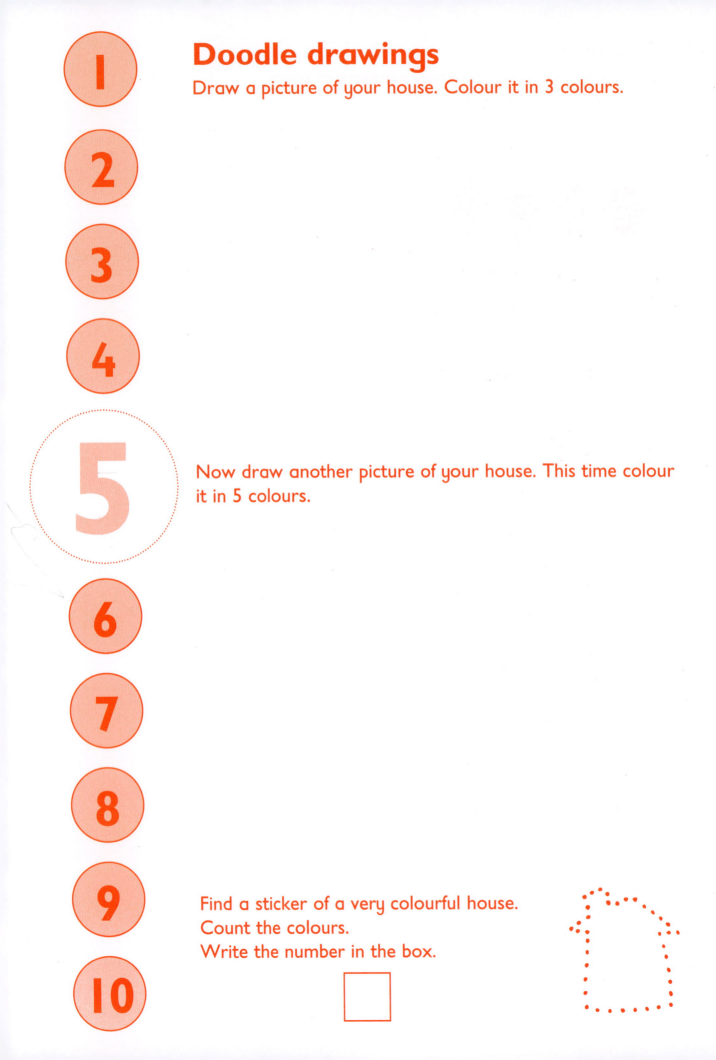

Doodle drawings
Draw a picture of your house. Colour it in 3 colours.

Now draw another picture of your house. This time colour it in 5 colours.

Find a sticker of a very colourful house.
Count the colours.
Write the number in the box.

Birds of a feather flock together

Birds that look the same want to be together.
Looks at these birds. Answer the counting questions.

How many birds...

...have long tails? ☐

...have short tails? ☐

...have curly tails? ☐

...have bushy tails? ☐

Which bird is all alone? Find a friend for it on the sticker page.

Well done! Put your reward sticker here.

Looking at shapes

Can you make a circle shape with your hands and fingers? Can you make a triangle shape?

Here are some names for different shapes.

square   circle   triangle   rectangle

Shapes all around

Find a sticker of a plate. What shape is it?
Draw a line to connect the plate to the matching shape.

Find a sticker of a window. What shape is it?
Draw a line to connect the window to the matching shape.

Robot shapes

Find a sticker of a robot's head.
Can you see the shapes that make up the robot?

Find square, circle, triangle and rectangle stickers.
Count the shapes in the robot picture. Write the numbers in the boxes.

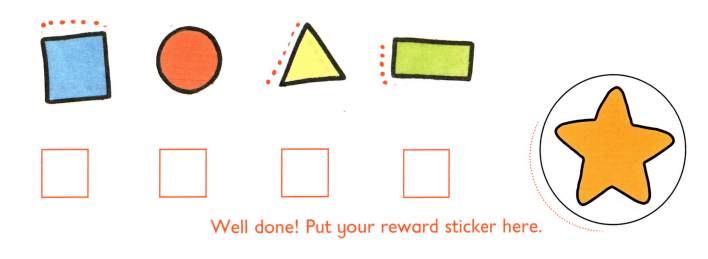

Well done! Put your reward sticker here.

Sorting shapes

Round shapes here. Square shapes there. There are shapes everywhere!

Colour the shapes with 4 sides yellow.
Colour the shapes with 3 sides blue.
Colour the other shapes red.

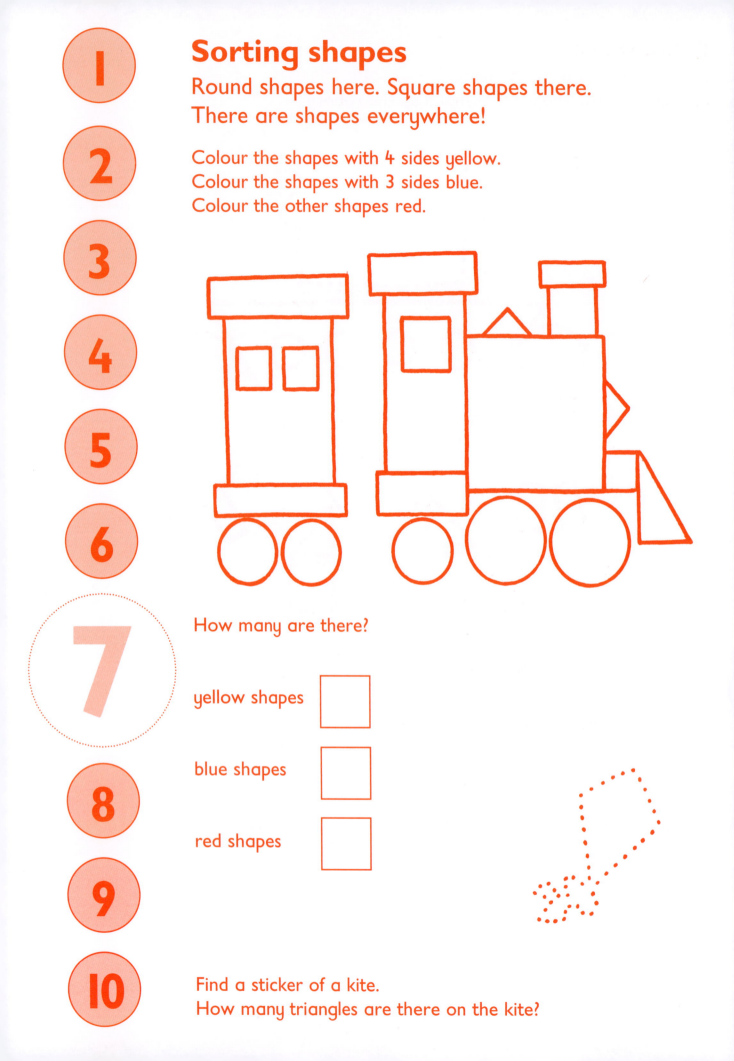

How many are there?

yellow shapes ☐

blue shapes ☐

red shapes ☐

Find a sticker of a kite.
How many triangles are there on the kite?

Terrible twins
Draw the missing shapes to make the robots the same.

Matching shapes
Colour the two shapes in each line that are exactly the same.

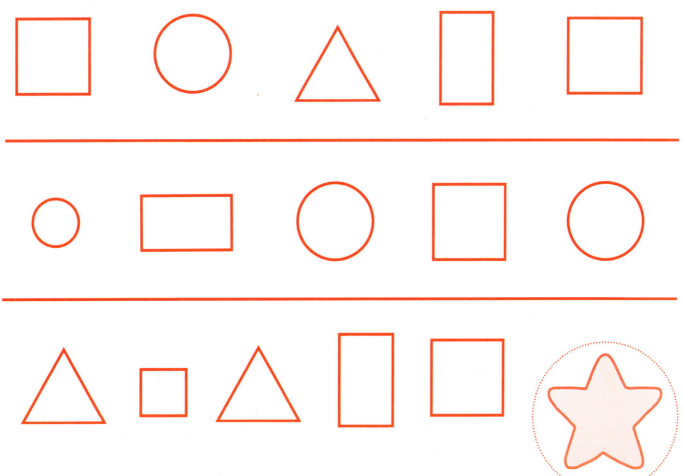

Well done! Put your reward sticker here.

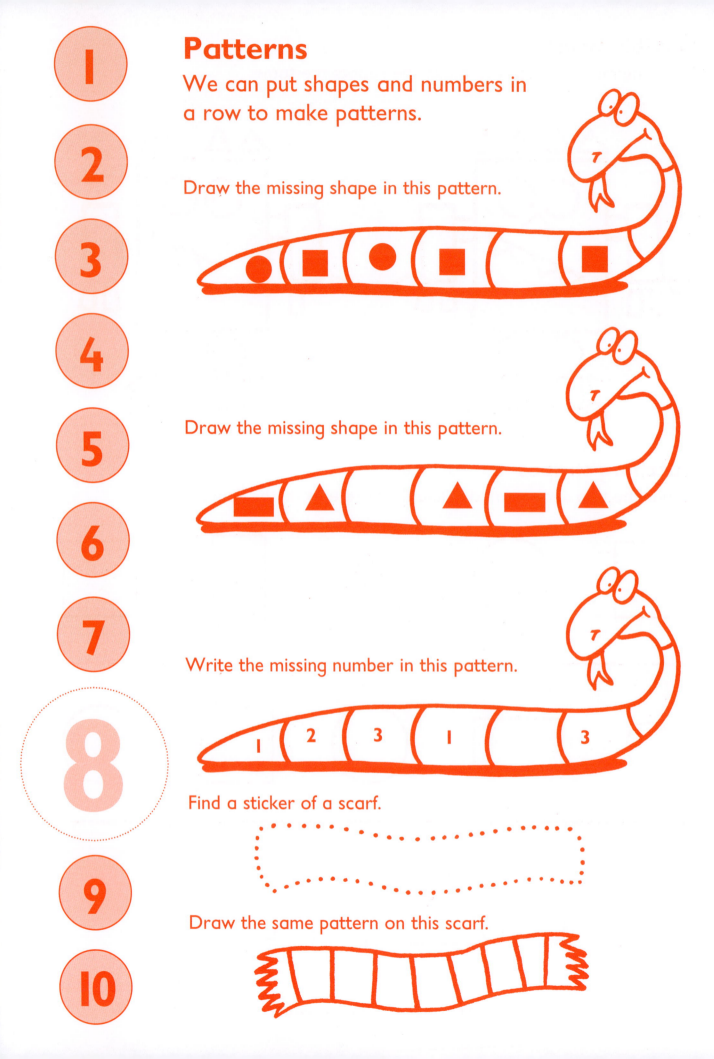

Same on both sides

Find a sticker of a butterfly wing.
Colour the other wing the same colours.

Finish the pictures

Trace the dotted lines to finish these shapes.

Well done! Put your reward sticker here.

What size?

When we want to know the size of something we measure it.

Find a sticker of a tree.
Which is the tallest tree? Colour it in.

Which is the longest log? Colour it in.

Smallest and shortest

Colour the smallest shoe.

Colour the shortest pencil.

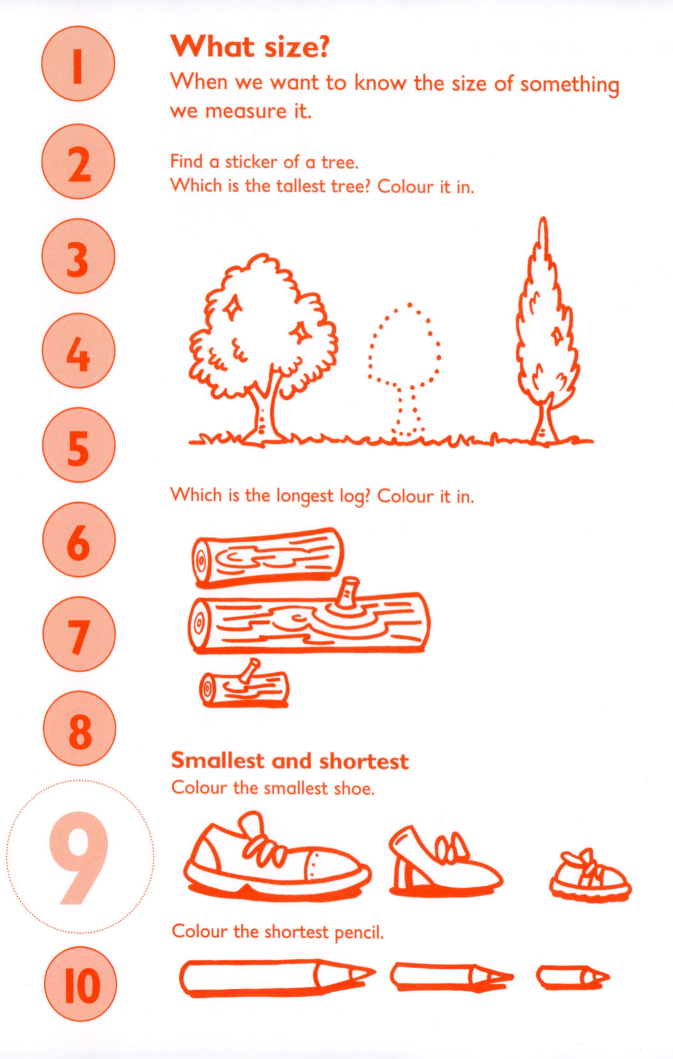

Fitting in

Find a sticker of a cereal box. How many cereal boxes can fit in the cupboard? Draw them.

Find a sticker of a van. How many vans fit in the car park? Draw them.

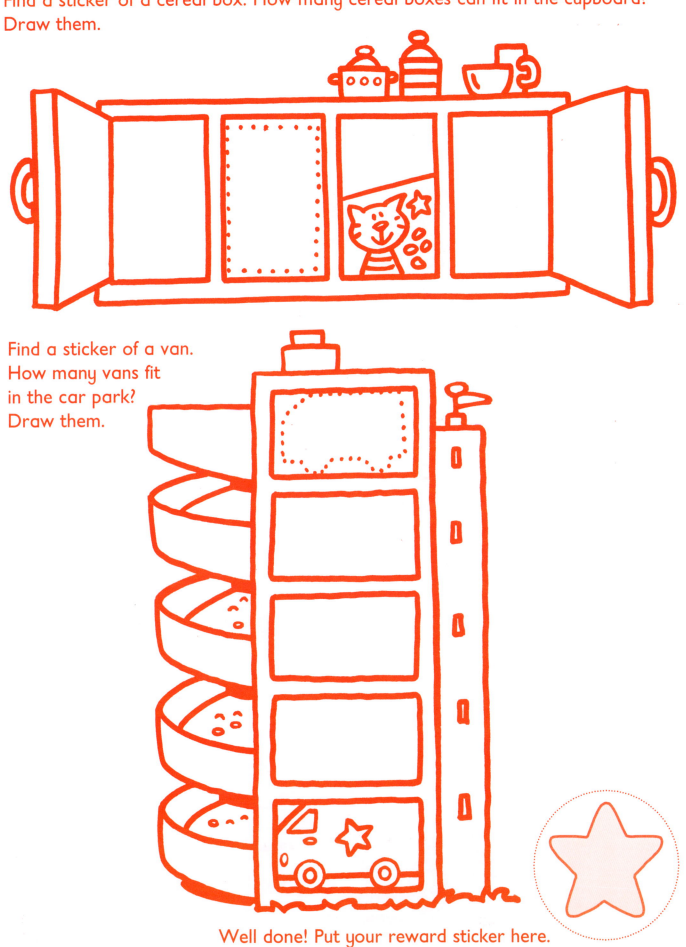

Well done! Put your reward sticker here.

First and last

Find a sticker to finish the picture.
Look for clues to tell you what the sticker might be.
In this picture story what comes first, what comes next, what comes last?
Write 1, 2 and 3 in the boxes.

Long time or short time?

How long does it take to do these things?
Which of these things take a short time? Which take a long time?
Draw a line from each picture to the 'short time' or 'long time' box.

Build a house.

Fly around the world.

Learn how to be a doctor.

short time

Grow a tree from a seed.

Eat an ice cream.

long time

Sing a song.

Watch your favourite TV programme.

Find a sticker of a clock.

Well done! Put your reward sticker here.

Adding sums

Here are some adding sums for you to try.
Count the pictures in each line and write the answer.

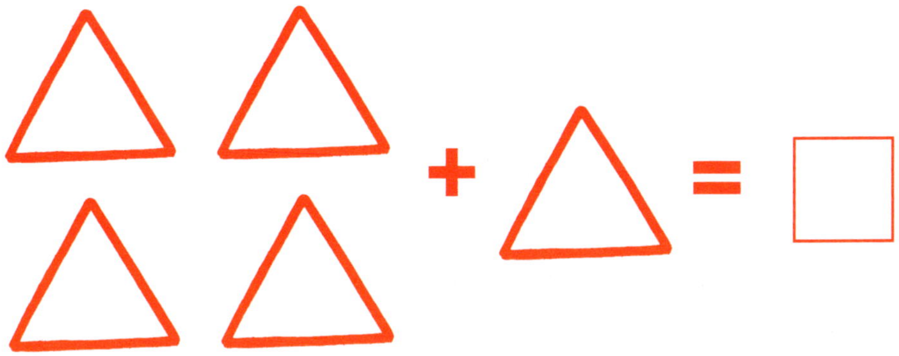

♡ + ♡♡♡ = ☐

🦆🦆 + 🦆🦆🦆 = ☐

🍦🍦🍦🍦 + 🍦🍦🍦 = ☐

🍎🍎🍎 + 🍎🍎🍎 = ☐

△△△△ + △△ = ☐

Well done! Put your reward sticker here.

Making 5

How many are there altogether? Write the answers in the boxes.

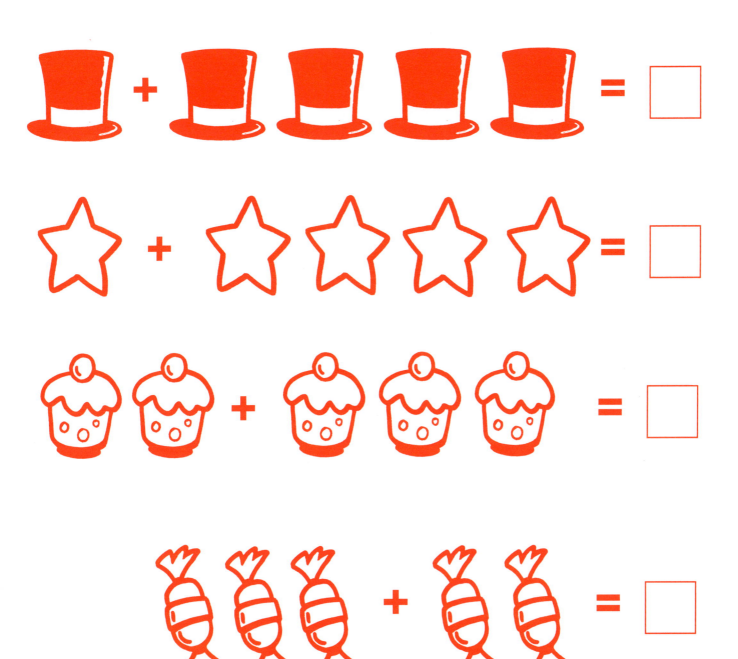

Find a rosette sticker.
The answer to the adding sums is on the rosette.
Were your adding sums correct?

Well done! Put your reward sticker here.

Five teds in a bed

This is a funny song. Can you learn it?

There were 5 in the bed and the little one said,
'Roll over, roll over.'
So they all rolled over and one fell out.

There were 4 in the bed and the little one said,
'Roll over, roll over.'
So they all rolled over and one fell out.

There were 3 in the bed and the little one said,
'Roll over, roll over.'
So they all rolled over and one fell out.

There were 2 in the bed and the little one said,
'Roll over, roll over.'
So they all rolled over and one fell out.

There was 1 in the bed and the little one said,
'Goodnight!'

Find a sticker of a ted in a bed.

Take away 2

Take away 2 things from each line by crossing them out.
How many are left?

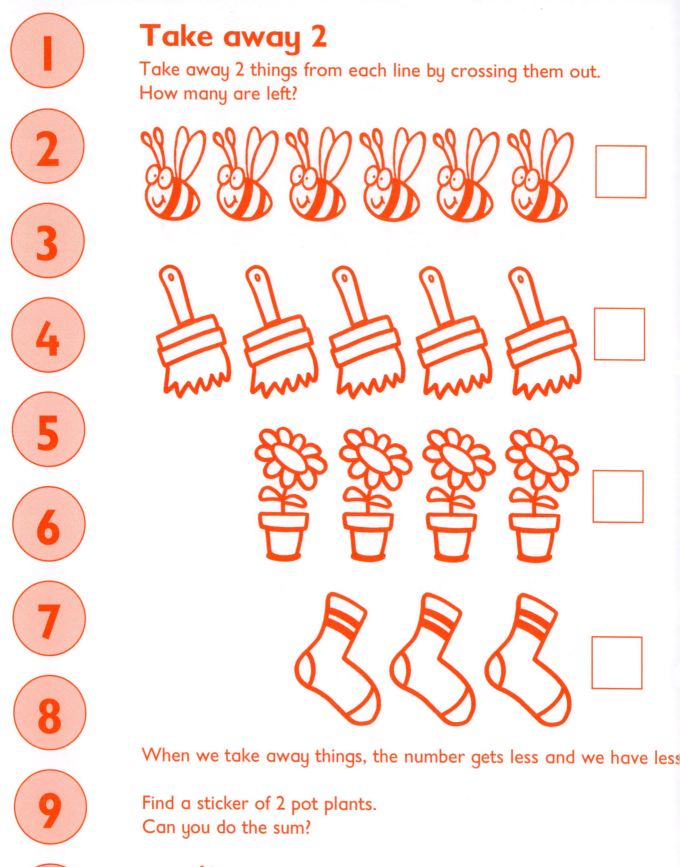

When we take away things, the number gets less and we have less.

Find a sticker of 2 pot plants.
Can you do the sum?

Take away 3

Here are some more take away sums. Take away 3 from each line. How many are left? Write the answer in the box.

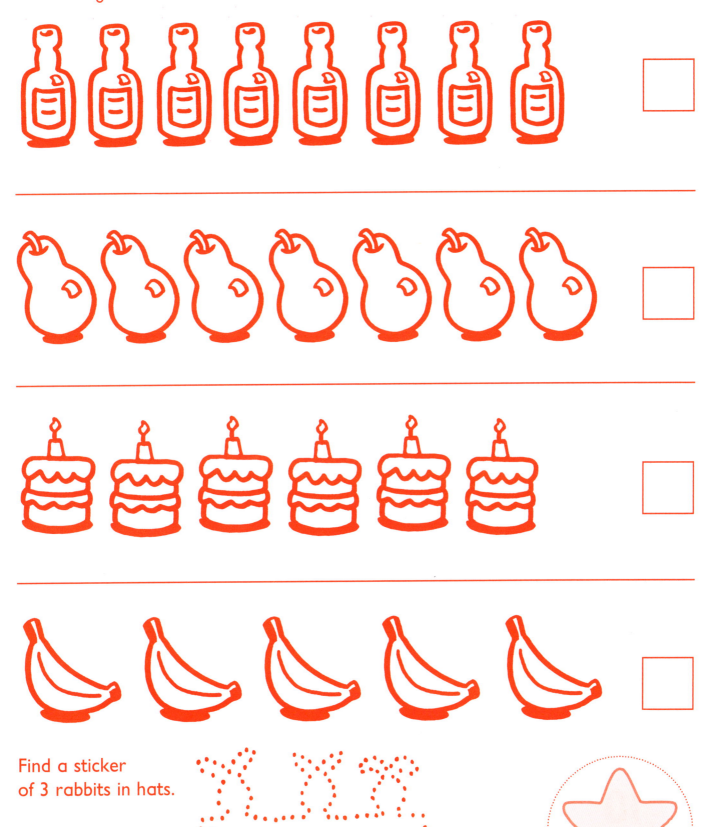

Find a sticker of 3 rabbits in hats.

Well done! Put your reward sticker here.

Sharing

Are there enough carrots for each rabbit to have 1 carrot?

Are there enough carrots for each rabbit to have 2 carrots? Circle two carrots and draw a line to each rabbit.

Find a sticker of 8 leaves.

How many leaves can each caterpillar have?

Multiply by 2 and 3

There are 3 children at a picnic. They each have 1 drink, 2 cakes and 3 sausages. Count the things in the picture.

☐ drinks   ☐ cakes   ☐ sausages

Find a sticker of a sausage.

There were 10 sausages in the pack and the children ate 9. How many sausages were left?

There was 1 sausage left. Can you guess who ate it?

Well done! Put your reward sticker here.

You are a star!

Find 5 triangles in the picture.
Colour these yellow.

Find 1 pentagon in the picture.
Colour it red.

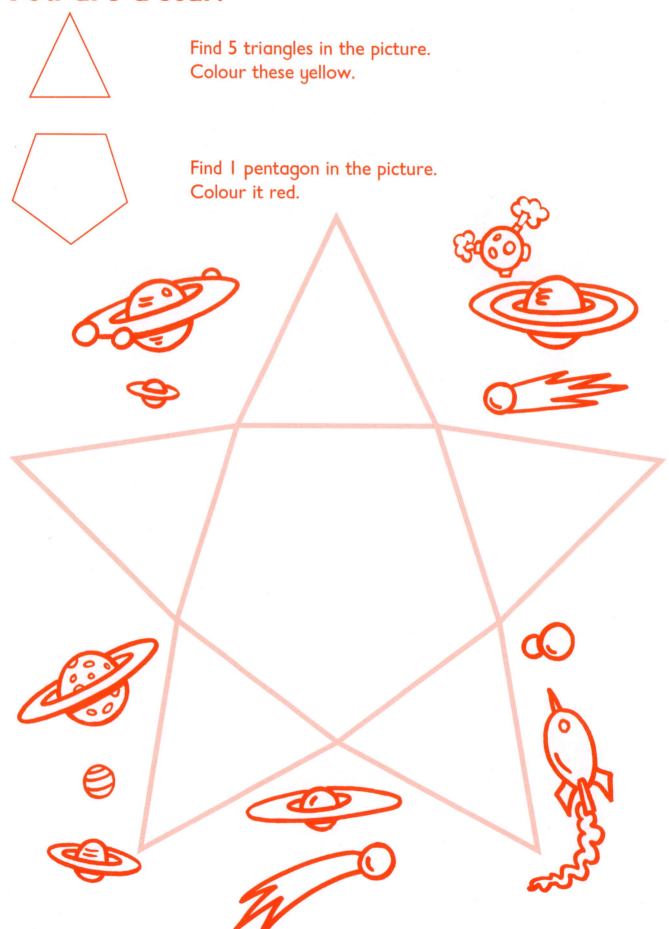

Well done! You are a star for finishing this book.